Tales of the Amazon

To Gabriela and Lucas, who grew up as Indians in spite of their real color.
To Tania, who took me on in spite of the difference.
To Walter Azevedo Tertulino, for his dedication to the Munduruku people.
To all, with love!

Text copyright © 1996 by Daniel Munduruku
Illustrations copyright © 1996 by Laurabeatriz
English-language translation copyright © 2000 by Jane Springer
Originally published in 1996 as *Histórias de indio* by Companhia das Letrinhas, São Paulo, Brazil
First English-language edition 2000

Groundwood Books/Douglas & McIntyre
720 Bathurst Street, Suite 500, Toronto, Ontario M5S 2R4

Distributed in the USA by Publishers Group West
1700 Fourth Street, Berkeley, CA 94710

We acknowledge the financial support of the Canada Council for the Arts, the Ontario Arts Council and the Government of Canada through the Book Publishing Industry Development Program for our publishing activities.

Canadian Cataloguing in Publication Data
Munduruku, Daniel, 1964-
Tales of the Amazon : how the Munduruku Indians live
"A Groundwood book."
Translation of: Histórias de indio.
Includes bibliographical references.
ISBN 0-88899-392-7
1. Munduruku Indians — Juvenile literature. I. Laurabeatriz. II. Springer, Jane. III. Title.

F2520.1.M8M8613 2000   j981'.0049838   C00-930400-2

Printed and bound in China by Everbest Printing Co. Ltd

Daniel Munduruku

Tales of the Amazon

How the Munduruku Indians Live

Illustrated by
Laurabeatriz

Translated by JANE SPRINGER

A Groundwood Book Douglas & McIntyre Toronto Vancouver Buffalo

Contents

Introduction

This book is about what life is like for some of the indigenous peoples of Brazil, many of whom live in the Amazon region. The information in the book is provided in different ways.

Part I is a story set in the midst of the Munduruku, the ethnic group of which I'm proud to be a member. It is the story of a child who is raised to be the religious leader of his Munduruku group in the Brazilian state of Pará. The story describes the journey the boy must make to succeed in his special training.

In Part II I describe how the Munduruku and various other Indian peoples live—their language, customs and clothing.

In Part III I tell you about myself and look back at some of the things that happened to me when I went to live in São Paulo—the biggest city in Brazil and one of the biggest in the world—which has a population of almost 20 million people. My experiences there raised questions that arise every day in encounters between Indians and city people.

In this section I ask many questions about how Indians and non-Indians live together. How do non-Indians look at the Indian who arrives in the city? How does an Indian experience the city?

I do not make any comment on these stories, but instead have left readers to come to their own conclusions. I hope the stories will also make you laugh—at the situation, at me and at yourselves.

—Daniel Munduruku

The Tale of the Boy Who Didn't Know How to Dream

THE CHOSEN ONE

The old pajé gazed with love at the child who had just been born. The shaman smiled as he thought about the great task that lay ahead. Soon he would educate this boy in the traditions of his people, in the art of healing, in his religion. He would teach the boy to speak with the spirits of the ancestors, teach him to guide his people with wisdom, honesty and a sense of justice, just as the pajé himself had done for many years.

This boy would be the guardian of a culture that had been carried from generation to generation. Through him, the ancestors would pass on the stories of the creation of the world. Through him they would speak to the people, who would follow his wisdom.

The old pajé smiled happily, filled with hope for the future of his people.

He called the boy's parents to him.

"My friends," he said, "listen carefully to what I am going to say. My heart is filled with happiness. The spirits of the wise ones have come to me in my dreams. They have told me that our people will live on, thanks to this baby who has been born today. He will be a blessing for our people, a great spirit who will speak with wisdom. But in order for this to happen, you must agree to let me educate him."

The parents looked at each other and smiled. They knew that this was a part of a tradition thousands of years old. They knew that to refuse the pajé's request would be to create discord in the universe.

"Our son is the son of this nation," they said to the old man. "Just as we are sons and daughters of this nation. We would not go against

the wishes of the Great Spirit. We will happily give you our son when the time comes."

Having said this, they took their leave. And the pajé lay in his hammock to dream and thank the ancestors.

THE NAMING

The pajé, Karu Bempô, watched the child grow up, rocked in his mother's loving arms. Once in a while he would go to the boy's house and gaze for a long time at the sweet face of his protégé. He remembered the day he had given the boy his name—a name that was inspired by the ancestors in his dream.

The pajé was walking in the middle of the bush, sheltered by the huge canopy of trees. It was very dark, and he could not see where he was going. He felt like resting but sensed the presence of the higher spirits, who said to him, "Pay attention. The canopy will open and reveal the name of the boy."

The pajé knew that the spirits would never let him down. He kept walking through the forest. Suddenly, he stopped. He felt a strange wind blowing above his head. He looked up and saw the moon shining in all its brilliance, as if it were smiling.

This must be the name of the boy, he thought—Kaxi, the moon that shines on humanity.

During the ceremony in which he named the boy, Karu Bempô said, "There are many bad forces that want to destroy our people. The white people, the pariwat, come to us with promises on the tips of their tongues.

They promise to uphold our traditions and customs. They say that they are friends of the Indians, that we are the true Brazilians and the most important inhabitants of this land. But then they destroy our people and our culture. They come with their so-called machines of progress, but the machines drown out our singing. They come with the paper that they call money, wanting to buy the souls of our people. They fool us with promises that bring sorrow and division into the hearts of our people. They pollute our rivers, destroy the spirits of our trees, drive out our cattle. Today we have to walk long distances if we want to eat the meat of our animals—the tapir, deer, wild pig, wild boar, monkey, raccoon. The pariwat have spoiled the banks of our Tapajós River, so we have to travel on other rivers if we want to find good fish. They have frightened our birds—the macaw, parrot, ibis, aro, pukaso.

"Even so, our people continue to grow stronger, because our tradition teaches us to struggle against the destruction brought by the pariwat."

Overcome with emotion, the pajé stopped talking for a moment and then continued, "Our people will never die out. The white man cannot destroy us. We will be reborn from the ashes if necessary. We will carry on our history and the memory of our brothers who have already died. On the day of humanity's final sunset, we, the children of the earth, will be sitting on the mountains watching it take place."

Having said this, the pajé lifted up tiny Kaxi and presented him to the community as the one who would guide the Munduruku people when the old man was reunited with the ancestors.

THE WAY OF LIFE

Until he was five years old, Kaxi's mother carried him everywhere with her. But as he grew up, he began to participate in the life of Katō village.

During the rainy season, he learned from his father how to handle the products of nature that could protect him when it was time for him to leave his parents' house. He gathered embira and bamboo leaves and learned how to make the containers that the women used to carry fruit and cassava. He learned how to make vine baskets, and his parents watched closely to make sure that he made them properly. When little Kaxi got completely mixed up with the knots he was making in the vines, everyone laughed while the oldest patiently explained the process to him.

Once Kaxi asked his father, "Papa, why is it

that when it rains, all of us come together here to learn crafts?"

"Son, when it rains, your mother cannot go to the field to pick cassava to make flour. We cannot fish or hunt, because the river rises and the fish hide between the tree roots, and it is hard to find them. The animals flee as well, looking for dry places to hide. They sometimes go so far away that it is too dangerous to venture into the forest to hunt them. When it rains, the snakes go into the clearings and they can attack us."

"Is that why we have less food at this time of year?"

"Yes. During the rainy season, there is less of our traditional food like game and fish. Instead we feed ourselves with flour, fruit and our chickens. Or we eat the food of the pariwat."

During the dry season between April and September, Kaxi would go with his mother to plant crops like cassava, sweet potatoes, bananas, maize, yams and sugarcane. The planting always took place after the bonfire, when the men cleared and burned a piece of land that the villagers called a ku. Each section of the ku had an owner who would plant whatever that family needed to live on.

During one of the burning days, Kaxi turned to his mother sadly and asked, "Mama, must we take down so many trees to plant cassava and other food? The trees seem to be crying with sadness."

"Kaxi," said his mother, "Nature suffers when people destroy it for no good reason. But we have no choice. If we don't cut down some trees to make our ku, we will die of hunger. If we plant our food beneath the trees, there won't be enough sun to heat the plants, and they won't grow and become strong. Life needs sun and water to maintain itself. That's why we plant now, while there is sun. Later, the rain will come to help our plants grow. Don't worry, little Kaxi. Mother Nature knows that we aren't doing this out of cruelty, but because we must in order to survive."

While the women took care of the ku and the household chores, the men hunted and fished, burned the brush and made bows and arrows that they used for hunting and fishing. They would also use them to defend the village if they had to. The men would meet at the end of every afternoon to talk about politics, and the pajé would tell stories about the marvelous acts of the heroes who had created humanity. They would tell jokes and laugh a lot among themselves.

Kaxi listened carefully to the men's stories. He learned about the contact between the Indians and the pariwat, which had brought so much misfortune to the tribe. He saw how the men's faces became very serious and sad when they talked about the terrible things the pariwat had committed against the people of other nations, how they had taken the wealth of their land. He also heard about white people who were friends of the Indians and who defended them against their enemies. He learned that the tribal leaders sought out these friendly people, hoping they could help combat the invaders of the sacred land of the Munduruku people.

Kaxi listened to these things, even though he did not understand them all. Often he slept

on his father's lap until the following morning.

Sometimes Kaxi would accompany the women on their walks through the forest looking for leaves to use as remedies. He came to know more and more about the healing powers of plants and herbs. He discovered that there was a plant for every illness. He learned to respect Nature, because he saw that she could not only cure all types of sickness, but could also wreak revenge on those who used her to satisfy their own interests. He developed a strong friendship with the trees and plants and told them he would take care of them with all his heart.

Kaxi also spent a large part of the day playing with the other children and his younger brothers and sisters. First thing in the morning he would gather the children together, and they would all go to the river to swim and play. He would take his tiny bow and arrow and set up a tournament, encouraging the other children to test their aim. The parents were happy to see the children play like this, because they knew such games made them strong and agile and helped them learn how to be part of a group.

After swimming and playing, the children would do some task with their mothers or fathers. There was no set time to begin this activity. Kaxi had heard that the pariwat used a watch to record the hours. But for Kaxi and his people, time could not be controlled. Sometimes they would go out very early to work in the ku or to hunt or fish. Other times they would only go in the afternoon. Some days they wouldn't go anywhere, preferring to stay at home talking and smoking.

When they returned from working with their parents, the children would get together again and talk about what they had done. One had gone fishing with his father. Another had gone to the field with her mother, carrying the basket with the cassava to the flour house. Another said that he had grated cassava to make bread and kneaded dough in the clay cylinder.

After everyone had spoken about what they had done, the children would go to the river and have a wonderful swim, making a huge uproar as they imitated the birds, monkeys and other animals. Then they would all meet and talk around the campfire that was burning in the center of the village.

Kaxi's people were very happy, living together in harmony with Nature. Kaxi knew that he was being instructed in the ways of his people.

His father had once told him that the pariwat learned about their way of life in a place called a school, and this gave them prestige and power over others. It meant they could get more of the heavy paper they called money. Kaxi thought this type of education was strange. How could someone learn how to make a snare or a bird trap shaped like a pyramid without going into the forest? Kaxi thought that it must be awful to learn like that, since the children had to stay away from their parents for a long time and would never learn how to dream.

RELIGIOUS RITUALS

As he grew up, Kaxi was initiated into the traditional customs of his people. He learned to speak the Munduruku language. He hunted, fished, planted and harvested with the adults. He learned about the history of his ancestors, about all the wars between the various groups, about the paintings and the body tattoos, about everything that was part of the culture of his nation.

Kaxi paid special attention to the various rituals that took place in the village. Most of these rituals were directed by the pajé: the naming of the children, the curing of serious illnesses, purification rites, wedding ceremonies, initiation rites of young people into adult life, the solemn moment of burying the dead. He learned that at each stage of life one must undergo a ritual of introduction to attain the good will of the community, justify the preparation for the new life phase, demonstrate one's ability to survive without one's parents and, especially, to receive the Great Spirit's blessing.

By the time Kaxi was ten years old, he had grown to see these rituals as extremely beautiful in the way they venerated the wisdom of the ancestors and reflected the traditions and ideals of his people. Like the others, he felt ecstasy when he took part in the rituals—there was no other way to describe it.

Kaxi had been going to rituals from the time he was born, but he did not always understand what he was seeing. So one day, after watching a curing session, Kaxi went up to Karu Bempô and asked, "Godfather, what were you doing to that woman's body?"

The pajé, tired because of the work he had been doing, smiled at the boy. "Little pajé, come to my hut tomorrow. But before you come, go to the forest and bring some leaves for me to smoke."

"Tomorrow I will be there when the sun is at its highest point," Kaxi answered.

That night, Karu Bempô had a strange dream. The pajé dreamt that he was a huge bird flying high above the Amazon. Below he could see huge clear-cut areas in the forest and machines that ate the trees. He saw the river become crimson because of the liquids that the pariwat were throwing into the water. He saw the forest crying and bleeding.

The pajé also flew over the lands of the neighboring peoples, both friends and enemies, and saw deterioration that grew worse the farther he went. He flew close to his people and saw that they were puzzled and frightened as the pariwat pressed closer. He saw his peo-

ple fleeing from their land, moving away from the sacred earth of the ancestors out of fear and without a spirit who could give them courage to fight for their land.

Frightened, the pajé shook himself out of his dream and woke up. He got up from his hammock and walked to the courtyard. As he gazed at each house in the village, he cried. He cried for the souls of the trees that had been destroyed. He cried because he was unable to help his people. And he knew that the time had come to prepare Kaxi's spirit to help his people to fight.

The following day, at noon, Kaxi stopped in front of the pajé's house and waited. He knew that a child could never rush an elder. Soon after, the pajé asked him to come in. Kaxi sat down while the pajé walked around the house smoking the leaves that Kaxi had brought. He threw out puffs of smoke as if he were purifying the space. In the room, a fire burned steadily and dully.

Karu Bempô came up to Kaxi and threw some puffs of smoke on the boy.

"Little pajé," he said, "it is time to tell you a secret. We are living in a fragile and dangerous time. Our people are at risk of dying off. There are others who want to destroy our culture, stealing the riches that make up the hair of our Mother Earth. The pariwat don't understand that they are breaking the heart of our mother when they clear-cut the forests to find gold. Our mother means nothing to them."

After a pause, the old man continued, "You know that our people have always been friendly with the pariwat and have always tried to help them. This has weakened our warrior spirit, and the white men have taken advantage of our weakness. They have contaminated our people, creating rivalries among us. Now we are suffering. We need someone who has the knowledge of the elders and the youth of the warrior, who can help us resist with courage.

The spirits of our ancestors have chosen you to be the leader. It is time for you to begin your instruction. You have much to learn and, most important of all, you must learn to dream."

Kaxi did not know what to say or to think. He had many questions. He knew, however, that when the pajé spoke, the spirits of the ancestors were speaking through him. Therefore there must be truth in what the wise old man was saying.

"What do I have to do?" the young Indian boy said finally.

"From now on, you will be under my supervision. I will be your guide and will pass on to you the knowledge you need to meet everything with courage and certainty."

"And my parents?"

"Your parents knew that this was going to happen."

"But why me?"

"I don't know," the pajé said dryly. "We don't decide our own destinies. We are guided by our ancestors, and often they make demands that we don't understand."

"Do I have the qualities I need to become a leader?" Kaxi asked.

"Everyone has. What is difficult is opening yourself up to learn correctly and willingly, and to know that what you are doing is not for yourself but for the whole community, which has put its trust in you."

Kaxi stood up and looked at the pajé affectionately.

"I am ready, Godfather," he said, "to do as the spirits wish."

THE INITIATION

And so the pajé began to initiate the boy in the traditional art of healing. "The pajé is a religious leader," he told Kaxi. "He presides over the most important rituals of the group because he is acting on behalf of the ancestors. Whoever hears the pajé hears the Great Spirit himself, accepts and follows his counsel. The pajé is a great energy in the village. Without him the wisdom of the ancestors falters and the people become weak and divided. You were chosen to be pajé in order to continue this tradition."

From that day on Kaxi went everywhere the pajé went. Often he would stay in the men's hut, thinking over the pajé's teachings. Karu Bempô told him that he should stay silent if he wanted to learn to speak with the spirits and be instructed by them.

Every day Kaxi learned new things. When he turned twelve, it was time to go through the rites of initiation into adulthood. He had to prove to the people that he was a man, that he was ready for marriage, that he was a warrior. The small pajé, called Small Moon by the others, knew that even though he had been chosen, he still had to pass this test of maturity in

order to gain adult status, to be a responsible man, courageous and mature. This would give him more stature among his people, and they would respect him.

For one whole month, Kaxi and twenty-four others were completely isolated from the village. They retired to the men's house, where they were initiated by their fathers and god-fathers in the art of hunting, fishing and survival in the bush.

The biggest test involved staying alone in the bush for several days and finding the means to survive. If a young man could do that, he would return home as a brave, bringing with him some large game that would provide food for the whole village. Kaxi knew that not all were able to achieve this goal the first time. Some had to return to the bush several times before they received the honors of the warrior.

After a month's retreat, the twenty-five

young men gathered in the center of the village. For a whole day they sang and danced, announcing their departure to the forest.

At daybreak, the pajé said, "Brave warriors, the moon is high in the sky. This is a good sign. It is time for the new warriors to leave for the forest and prove that they are worthy of belonging to this nation. You will encounter many dangers and traps set by Mother Nature to test your strength, but remember that Nature is your sister and not your enemy. If you talk to her in the proper way, she will not leave you without an answer. Have courage. Go with the Great Spirit."

A deafening silence fell on the village. The young men knew that it was time to leave. They went into the bush without looking back, so as not to see their mothers' eyes, full of joyful tears.

IN THE FOREST

During the first days of the journey, the group stayed together. But as they went deeper and deeper into the forest, the young Indians began to distance themselves from each other. They all knew that tradition spoke of the warrior's individual courage and that the more alone they were, the more courageous they would be.

Kaxi separated himself from the group. After six days without encountering any animals to eat, he heard someone calling him from a clearing in the forest. Exhausted, he hung his hammock between two trees and lay on his back looking up at the stars. Then he closed his eyes.

He remembered the day when Karu Bempô

had told him that he had been chosen to be the pajé, the keeper of the nation's knowledge, guardian of the wisdom of the people, protector of their traditions.

He remembered the pajé's words: "To be a good pajé you must learn to dream."

"I don't know how to dream," Kaxi had replied.

"Everyone dreams," the pajé had said. "But few people know what they dream and still fewer know how to interpret their dreams. You already dream. I will make you a remedy so that you can keep the dreams that you have in your memory."

Kaxi remembered that the remedy was very simple. The pajé had gone to the forest to find some ants and, without disturbing their activities, had carefully gathered up their droppings in a small box. He put them in the sun for a few days until they were completely dry. Then the pajé rubbed them in Kaxi's hair.

While he was doing this, the pajé said in a very low voice, "Dream, my son. It is the oldest form of learning that our people have. We held out in many battles because we knew how to listen to the voices of the ancestors who speak to us in dreams. Through dreams we

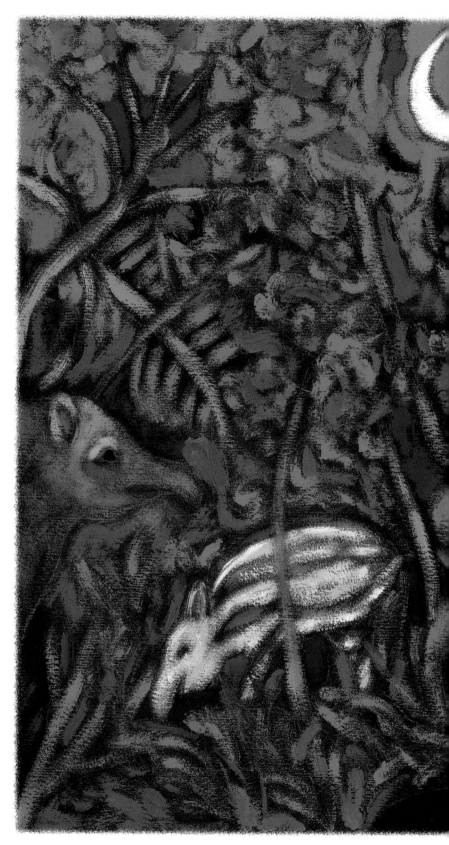

can see farther, hear more clearly, travel long distances and recognize danger. But dreaming is not a privilege, it is a necessity. The pajé is the official interpreter of the community's dreams. Without him to explain the significance of dreams, the spirit of the community becomes weak and can easily be vanquished by enemy forces."

"But, Godfather, if I never manage to interpret my own dreams, how will I be able to interpret the dreams of others?"

"Don't worry, my boy. You are not the first to have this difficulty, and certainly you will not be the last. This remedy will help you learn how to dream. One day, when it is time, you won't even need to have people tell you their dreams. You will only have to look at a person to know what he or she is dreaming. As you know, there are other people in our community who are said to be pajés because they possess this power, but they use it to satisfy their own interests, to dominate others. You must be careful how you use this gift."

Kaxi also remembered one night when he and the pajé had gone out to gather plants at the edge of the forest. Kaxi, who had already learned a lot about plants from his mother, went some distance away from the pajé to gather them. When he returned, his godfather was singing a sad song. He said he was reaching the moment when he would meet with the ancestors and live beside the Great Spirit.

Kaxi saw that an intense light surrounded the pajé while he was singing. The old man called out to the boy. When Kaxi asked how he had guessed his presence, the wise man answered that a pajé never guesses, he knows.

"I am ready to travel to another reality. I

will be with the ancestors and I will continue to be present among you, but even so I leave with sadness that I have not done more for my people. But I am also full of joy and hope to know

that I leave the people in good hands, because you are a great disciple and friend, capable of huge sacrifices for your people. This is what one expects of a pajé."

The next day, Kaxi had asked to know more about the function of a religious leader. Karu Bempô had answered with great patience.

"A pajé is like a savior, a healer, a prophet. He cures the wounds of the body, because illnesses are bad spirits, cauxi, that inhabit the bodies of the sick. The pajé also cures the hidden wounds at the base of the soul. He tries to unite that which is disunited, light the fire that has gone out in the heart, speak the words of the Great Spirit. The pajé, my son, shows the way. The pariwat think that the pajé is a liar, a trickster, because he uses remedies from the forest to cure the body. They think sicknesses come from bad food, from tiredness, from worry. They say that evil comes from the outside. We, the pajés, believe that illness enters into the soul itself to lead a person away from the path of the Great Spirit."

Kaxi's hammock rocked in a slow but constant rhythm as his conversations with the pajé flooded his thoughts.

"When you return from the forest, I will no longer be here, but my heart will accompany

you always. While you are proving your courage, the Great Spirit will take me to be with him. But I will continue to protect and teach you. Everything is all right. You are already prepared. This is your moment."

Kaxi did not understand exactly what the pajé's farewell meant. It made him feel weak and lonely. He hadn't yet learned how to dream. How could he take the place of the wise pajé? How would he ever live up to such a responsibility?

THE DREAM

Rocked by the silence of Mother Nature, Kaxi seemed to feel Karu Bempô saying to him, "This is your moment." Then he fell asleep, and he dreamed.

In his dream he met his godfather, who guided him along the paths of the dream. Kaxi entered the spirit of a jakora, a wild cat of the Amazon forest. He ran for a long time down a wild, unruly trail. He went to the heart of the world and saw where the game hid. He went to the end of the earth and saw men and machines destroying trees, digging up the soil.

He turned into an eagle and flew high above the rivers. He was a snake and crawled through the canopies of the trees. He entered into the spirits of the trees and heard their laments, their cries of sorrow over their siblings who had been destroyed by the people's greed. He changed into a fish and felt the sorrow of the rivers whose waves were now filled with waste, garbage and filth.

In his dream Kaxi also felt the uneasiness of his brothers and sisters in his community. He saw that contact with the pariwat had made his society a place of death and sorrow. He saw many brothers using clothes to cover their bodies, ashamed to walk in harmony with Mother Earth. He saw many whose eyes were fascinated by the technology of the white man, watching the box that spoke and lied. He saw a fight between two brothers over the heavy paper, the cause of envy and greed. He saw his people ashamed to believe in the Great Spirit and in his teachings.

He looked into the center of his village and saw a cross and understood that the Great Spirit had been banned by men with black clothing and women in white. He saw many people kneeling before the cross and lining up to receive bread. He saw brothers and sisters who were afraid of dying because they felt guilty about being born as "savages." He entered the body of one of his people and heard him repeating the lies of the non-Indian to save his soul.

The small pajé went into the center of a men's house and saw many strong warriors drinking a fire water that left them outside themselves. He saw white men bringing this water and negotiating to buy their land. In truth, they wanted to buy their souls.

Kaxi returned to his own body. When he awoke, he cried because of everything he had seen. He felt weak and battered, as if many days had passed. He was hungry. Strangely, however, he felt he had the power to remember what he had dreamed. He also sensed that he could understand everything he had seen in his dream.

At this moment Kaxi saw a huge clearing in the forest with marvelous lights hovering in the air around it. He saw a familiar face smiling at him. It was Karu Bempô, his godfather.

In the face of such happiness, seeing himself as the keeper of centuries-old knowledge, Kaxi felt his legs go weak. Suddenly, everything around him seemed to spin, and he fainted.

Kaxi woke up a few hours later. His tiredness was gone. He sat on the edge of his hammock and thought about everything he had

seen and felt. It was amazing to be able to see with such clarity the things that he must do to fulfill the great mission he had to accomplish together with his people. He was pleased with himself for having learned how to dream. He felt complete and unified with the spirit of the old pajé who had passed all his knowledge on to him.

In this spirit of gratitude, Kaxi realized that it was time to return to his people. But he was hungry, and he still had to find some game to give to the community. He went in search of animals. He found a herd of tapir and took pride in aiming and hitting one of them right in the heart. He made a small litter to transport it. Then he saw a small rodent called an aguti that was searching for food. Kaxi shot an arrow at the animal and killed it. He lit a fire, cooked the meat and ate tranquilly but voraciously. Then he put his bow and arrow on his back and set off for his village.

He had fulfilled his apprenticeship with his dear godfather Karu Bempô. Now it was time to begin a mission that was even more difficult —to guide his people toward their future...

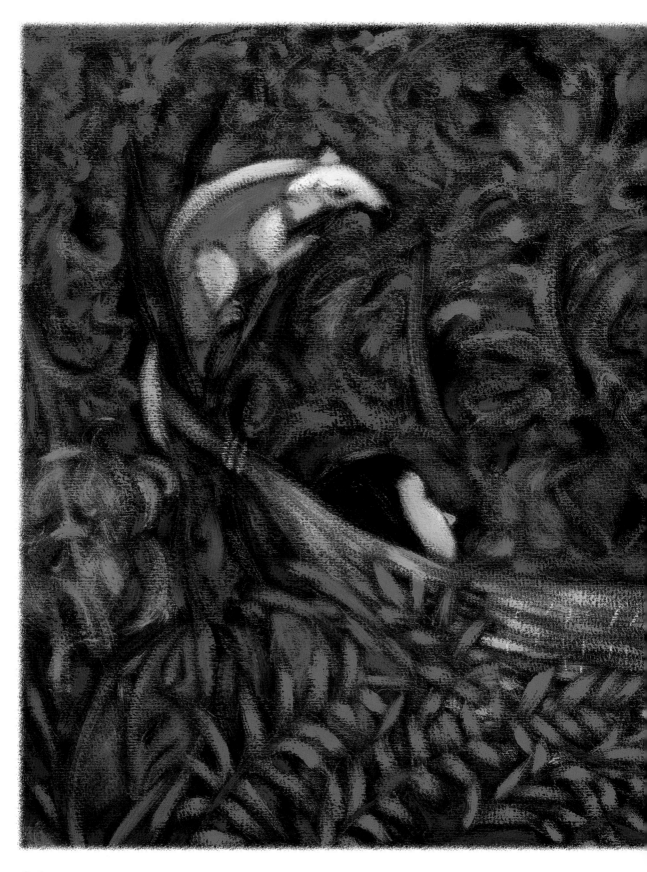

EQUATOR

Negro

Amazon

Manaus

Tapajós

Xingu

PARÁ

Belém

Porto Velho

BRAZIL

Brasília

Belo Horizonte

São Paulo

Rio de Janeiro

ATLANTIC OCEAN

CANADA
UNITED STATES
MEXICO

CUBA
HAITI
DOMINICAN REPUBLIC
PUERTO RICO
JAMAICA

BELIZE
GUATEMALA
HONDURAS
EL SALVADOR
NICARAGUA
COSTA RICA
PANAMA

COLOMBIA
ECUADOR
VENEZUELA
GUYANA
SURINAM
FRENCH GUIANA
PERU
BRAZIL
BOLIVIA
PARAGUAY
CHILE
URUGUAY
ARGENTINA

The Indigenous Peoples
of Brazil

The Munduruku

ALDO PARAWÁ

ONÉSIMO DATIÉ

The Munduruku are only one of more than two hundred indigenous peoples in Brazil. They live in an area in the state of Pará that is bordered by the banks of the Tapajós River and its estuaries. There are eighty-six villages inhabited by about 5,500 people, according to FUNAI; the Brazilian Federal Agency for Indian Affairs.

The Munduruku have maintained a large part of their traditional culture in spite of more than 150 years of contact with Brazilian society. The Munduruku language belongs to the Tupi linguistic branch and is considered by the tribe to be the main indication of the difference between them and the world of whites. Everyone speaks Munduruku in the area. Only the youngest know how to speak Portuguese, Brazil's national language, which they have learned in schools in their villages or through contact with the "civilized" people who live in the surrounding areas.

The Munduruku live from hunting, fishing and collecting fruit, and they farm and raise domestic animals such as chickens, cattle, ducks and sheep. They also mine gold and grow rubber and cashews.

The Munduruku village consists of a line of houses constructed out of timber and tied with vines. There is always a large area between the houses where the children can play. The whole village is built close to a river, where the people can fish and leave cassava to soak before it can be turned into flour, the main food of the Munduruku and many other indigenous groups of the Amazon.

Every village has a chief, who is called the captain. He makes the decisions after hearing the views of the people in the community. In the past, every village also had a religious leader or pajé, but today there are few real pajés left.

The Munduruku believe that they were created by the Great Spirit, whom they call Karu Sakaibö. Many myths describe the adventures of this hero. A myth is a story about gods that attempts to explain why life is the way it is. Every people has its myths. Even "western civilization" was developed with the myth of Adam and Eve.

The Munduruku are divided into two large families, each of which is called a half. One half is red, the other white. The people in each color have certain surnames, and the people who belong to one color cannot marry another person of the same color. For example, someone with the surname Datié, Akai, Krixi, Boron, Ikon, Tawé, Puxu or Tonhon (who belong to the white half) can only marry someone with the surname Kabá, Karu, Waru, Panhon or Krepon (who belong to the red half). Anthropology—a science that studies human cultures—calls this exogamous marriage. This division is explained in an ancient myth that helps the Munduruku to organize themselves socially.

Today the Munduruku are facing many serious problems that could destroy their culture. There is a great deal of wealth on Munduruku land and in their rivers. People want to exploit the forests, the gold, the iron and other resources. The result is that the federal government, under pressure from business interests, has put off placing a border around the land, and has let non-Indians come into the area.

WALDILEIA CAETANO KABÁ

ONÉSIMO DATIÉ

SIMAR KURAP

51

From Pará to Brazil

FLÁVIO WARÚ

In Brazil, there are many different ways of life. In São Paulo, for instance, the largest city in Brazil, there are people from all over the world— Koreans, Japanese, Chinese, Portuguese, Italians and others. Each group values its own culture and forms a colony, following its own religious traditions, language, food and way of dressing. The people of São Paulo accept these different customs, and the newcomers become part of the life of the city.

The total population of Brazil is 160 million, of which 300,000 are Indians. They are called Indians because they lived in the area when Europeans "discovered" it in 1500 and thought they had arrived in India. At that time there were an estimated 5 million indigenous people belonging to almost one thousand different ethnic groups.

Throughout Brazil's history, many people were exterminated because of the Europeans' greed, so that only about two hundred groups have survived. They are very different from one another, and they relate to nature in various ways to secure their survival. To think of one Brazilian Indian group that forms a single nation would be the same as seeing the Italians, Russians and French as a single nation.

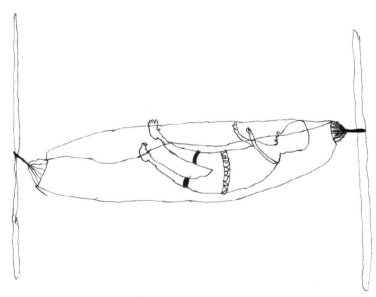

ALDILO

Linguistic Diversity

One of the most important elements of a people's culture is language. Many people believe that all Indians in Brazil speak Tupi, because the Portuguese conquerors singled out this language when they encountered people all along the Brazilian coast who spoke it. The missionaries learned and disseminated Tupi, making it the best-known Indian language in Brazil. Writers also gave more emphasis to Tupi.

The first classification of Brazil's languages was done by the early colonizers and missionaries, who followed the distinctions made by the Tupi people. Thus there were the Tupi and the Tapuya—people who didn't speak Tupi and therefore were considered to be barbarians or foreigners.

VALDEMIRA AKAY

Today the term Tapuya no longer has any meaning. Naturalist Von Martius demonstrated that the so-called Tapuya were not a homogenous group—some people who were considered to be Tapuya had nothing in common with others in the same category. Eventually many language groups were recognized, such as Tupi, Jê, Karib and Aruak, as well as minor groupings such as Pano, Tukano, Guaikuru and Maku.

It is important to remember that there are more than 170 languages and indigenous dialects spoken today in Brazil. Some people in the same region speak three different dialects. There are also groups that no longer speak their native language because of their dependence on non-Indians, and speak only Portuguese, the national language of Brazil.

Cultural Diversity

Language is only one example of the great diversity that exists among the indigenous peoples of Brazil. The Brazilian Indian does not have a uniform way of life. Some groups that live in the same or adjoining geographic areas may share similar cultural traits such as religion, language, food, farming practices, clothing, art, dances and celebrations. However, there are also many examples of cultural differences.

ALDO POXO

HOUSES

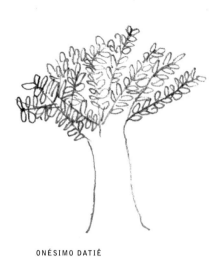

ONÉSIMO DATIÊ

L arger communities consist of a group of houses that are arranged in a variety of ways. Different groups call their houses by different names. The Indian house often illustrates the role that each person occupies in the society and what his or her obligations, duties and rights are within it.

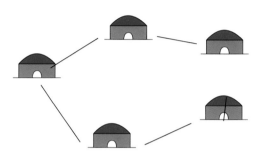

For example, in central Brazil, there are often circular villages where family dwellings are arranged around a central plaza. This is how the Kamayura, Bororo and Krahô indigenous groups live.

ALDO POXO

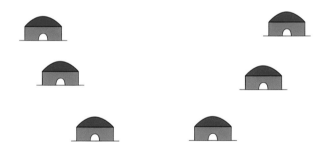

In rectangular villages, houses are arranged in a U formation. The Surui villages in the Amazon region are set up like this.

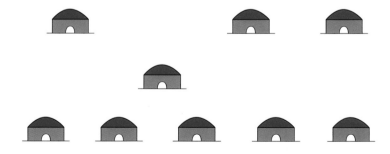

ONÉSIMO DATIÊ

And in linear villages the houses are organized in lines. Munduruku houses are set up like this, in two rows.

MARRIAGE

Although there are a number of common ways that villages organize their houses, it is very difficult to describe common types of marriage, since they vary a great deal. However, there is one common characteristic. Indians marry relatives according to well-defined rules. For some groups, like the Suruí, the ideal marriage is between a man and his sister's daughter—that is, his niece. For other tribes, it is good for cousins to marry. Each indigenous nation has its own ritual for the marriage ceremony, which ends in a huge party celebrating the continuity of their people. Some also accept marriages of a man with more than one woman or a woman with more than one man.

AMARILDO KABÁ

MYTHS

Myths are fantastic ways of explaining how the world began. It is through myths that people explain the origin of the universe, day and night, health and sickness, the sun, the moon, life and death—everything that makes up the lives of people in a community. To understand myths you need to have some knowledge of the people to whom they belong. They may say a lot to a particular people but to others they may mean nothing. Their function is not to give a scientific explanation but to make sense of everything and relate it to the social life of the people.

DIMAS WARÚ

Most indigenous myths portray animals as being responsible for various transformations in the history of humankind. Many myths speak of a time when the jaguar was the keeper of fire and people ate only raw food. A bird stole the fire from the jaguar to give it to the people, who then learned to put it to their own use. The myths that speak of the origin of humankind almost never begin from nothing. They usually tell the story of an original being who created all things and then taught people how to use them.

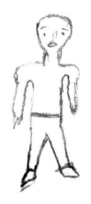

AMARILDO KABÁ

MARRIAGE AMONG THE BORORO

Among the Bororo Indians the young woman almost always takes the initiative of declaring her desire to marry the young man of her choice. She prepares a meal and, at noon, goes to the hut where the young man lives, accompanied by her mother. The mother gives the young man the food, saying, "My son-in-law, I came here with my daughter who wants to live with you because she loves you."

Normally the young man does not respond right away. He continues to work as if nothing has happened. After the young woman and her mother leave, the young man makes a decision. If he wants to marry her, he tastes the food she has offered. If he doesn't want to marry her, he doesn't eat it. Then it is up to his mother to return the dish full or empty to the mother of the young woman.

Sometimes it is the young woman herself who takes the food to the young man of her choice, inviting him to live with her. After a few days, if he wants to marry her, the young man goes hunting. He takes the animal that he has killed to his mother, who cooks it and offers it to the young woman. With this gift of food, the young woman knows that she has been accepted as his wife. The same day, the mother of the young man paints and decorates the young woman's body, tying her wrists with pieces of cotton, the sign of a married woman. The young woman returns to her mother's house and lights a bonfire— around which her new family will live.

Some indigenous societies do not mark marriage with any special ritual, or they keep it to a minimum. Among the Tenetehara, for example, once a marriage is arranged—a choice in which the head of the young woman's family is actively involved, because they want a son-in-law who is a worker—the bridegroom moves to the bride's house with his belongings. They sleep together right from the beginning, unless she is still a girl.

Júlio César Melatti, *Índios do Brasil*, São Paulo, Hucitec, 1993, pp. 126-27.

ELIANE DATIÉ

MUSIC

For indigenous people, every important event is a reason for the community to dance and commemorate it. But no celebration can take place without music. So all Brazilian indigenous groups have developed a way of expressing themselves musically. Some make flutes of various types and sizes, using material from the forest. Others make maracas or small bracelets that rattle when they are shaken.

The main instrument of indigenous peoples, however, is the body itself. Indians yell raucously, clapping their hands or feet in a perfect rhythm that puts the participants in harmony with themselves and with nature.

Through music, Indians teach their children about the ancient traditions of their people. Through the music that has been passed down through the centuries, people hear both their own voices and the voices of the gods.

AMARILDO KABA

WORK

We often hear that Indians are lazy, but Indians are hard workers. When the colonizers tried to get Indians to work to produce things for them, they discovered that the Indians weren't used to being told what to do. So they came up with the idea that Indians don't like to work. Then the colonizers hunted and killed the Indians who didn't adapt to the rhythm of slave work.

In fact, indigenous people spend many hours a day working at activities to provide their food and to support their traditions and culture. When non-Indians talk about work, they think first about getting money and goods. When Indians talk about work, they think of the livelihood of the people they are responsible for. Indians do not need to accumulate goods to become rich. On the contrary, the sign of wealth in an Indian community is generosity. The more generous the head of a family is, the richer his people consider him to be.

However, in order for someone to be considered generous,

SIMAR KURAP

they must possess goods, and those goods can only be acquired if an individual works diligently. So if someone wants to be considered generous—and that's the ideal of all Indians—they must work hard. There is not much specialization of work among the Indians. Each Indian knows how to do everything, and no one person knows more than any other. The main division that exists is between men's work (hunting, fishing, making bows and arrows, preparing the land) and women's work (spinning, sewing, cooking, gathering fruit, weaving).

RELIGIOUS CHIEFS

The pajés are the religious leaders who maintain the harmony of the group. They are responsible for keeping the group united, healthy and in balance. They must identify the evil spirits and try to fight them by praying, singing, chanting or calling for help. It is the pajés who converse with the supernatural. In some groups, they have the power to cure. They know the best remedies and the plants that can cure each illness. These wise men are consulted about the best path to follow in life, because they visit the gods in their dreams and know how to act in times of greatest difficulty.

SIMAR KURAP

STAGES OF LIFE

In indigenous communities each stage of life requires a special ritual. People mark every passage, from birth to death. These rituals are taken very seriously. A person from outside might be astounded to see young boys and girls shut in large huts for days and sometimes even months—without seeing the sun, totally enclosed, waiting for the day when they can return to the community. This takes place, for example, when a child reaches adolescence or when girls menstruate for the first time, when a woman has a child or when someone gets married, when people are sick or in mourning after someone's death. Each moment in the life of the community is greeted with a striking ritual to emphasize a sense of belonging to the group and obeying its social norms.

SIMAR KURAP

POLITICAL ORGANIZATION

The history of indigenous resistance began a long time ago. Indians have never accepted being mistreated by the European invaders, and this situation has not changed much since 1500. Many Indians died and many continue to die, and there are still conflicts over land between Indians and non-Indians. In fact, at times there is much more violence now than in the past, since Indians no longer expect the government to protect them. Instead they are protecting themselves. It is common to hear that Indians from a certain region have kidnapped and are holding people prisoner to call attention to their problems.

AMARILDO KABÁ

But the indigenous peoples have found another way to make the authorities aware of their situation. In the 1970s, Indians began to take part in the political life of Brazil by running for office in the National Congress. Their first victory was the election of Mário Juruna, a Shavante Indian.

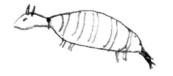

SIMAR KURAP

The Indians have also created the Union of Indigenous Nations (UNI), representing more than eighty different ethnic groups. Other organizations have also emerged. Although there is still a lot to be done, today almost all indigenous peoples belong to a group or association that fights for their rights and exerts political pressure on their behalf.

Current Problems of the Indigenous People

The Indians are not living in paradise. In fact, indigenous people will continue to face serious problems of survival if the real value of their very different but very human culture is not recognized. Indians have always been children of the earth. It is in the sacred soil of Mother Earth that they carry on their traditions. It is in the hair of Mother Earth that they find their nourishment, take the raw materials to build their houses, make their bows and arrows, bury their dead, celebrate life. However, these are the things that are most threatened by non-Indians.

ELIANE DATIÊ

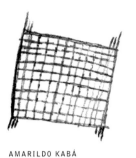

AMARILDO KABÁ

According to the 1988 Constitution, within a five-year time frame, all the indigenous areas in Brazil were to be set apart and officially recognized to be under government protection. Yet in practice, Indians still do not have the right to the land that they have occupied for hundreds of years.

Some people say that there is a lot of land in Brazil but very few Indians, and that the ideal would be to group them together on a small parcel of land. Others claim that Indians are holding back the development of the Brazilian nation because they don't want their land to be exploited for its riches. We know, however, that this is not true, when a few companies already occupy a million hectares of the Amazon region. Lumber companies, for example, want to buy lumber at a low price and export it at a high one. These companies are responsible for deforesting an enormous area of the Amazon, harming the environment and the people who inhabit it. Like all human beings, Indians can be fooled by companies that promise them rivers of money in exchange for lumber. Because they are not used to dealing with money, the Indians sometimes lose everything and end up living in poverty—and, what is worse, without the trees that are necessary for their survival.

Miners and prospectors are also invading indigenous areas. Looking for easy riches, they pollute the rivers, killing fish,

INDIGENOUS RIGHTS OF THE 1988 CONSTITUTION

AMARILDO KABÁ

The federal Constitution of 1988 was a landmark in the history of indigenous peoples in Brazil. It established that the Indians of Brazil have an original right to the land they traditionally occupy. Indigenous peoples were also guaranteed respect for their social organization, customs, languages, beliefs and traditions. For the first time ever, Indians' right to be Indians was recognized.

These changes were brought about by the tremendous effort of Indians, anthropologists, lawyers and activists throughout the country.

While the 1988 Constitution provides the legal basis for Indians' claims, there is still much to be done. The task of guaranteeing respect for indigenous rights in practice still lies ahead.

Source: Instituto Socioambiental

bringing disease and provoking armed conflicts between Indians and non-Indians. The federal government is often responsible for these incursions, because they authorize the exploitation of the ore without the consent of the people who will be affected by it.

The workers who come to build roads are another problem for the Indians. Once they establish themselves on land held by the Indians, they act as if they own it. This, of course, creates conflicts.

Hydroelectric companies are also guilty. Electric power stations are built on indigenous land and have been responsible for the extermination of whole human populations in the last thirty years, since they cover very rich cultural areas. Yet the government itself states that dozens of power stations will be built on indigenous land over the next ten years.

CLAUDINEIA AKAY

Classification of Groups

There are four types of indigenous peoples in Brazil.

Isolated: These are hostile or remote groups living in hard-to-reach areas or people who have fled from contact with the national population. We know this from the traces that they have left when they move from place to place. According to the Socio-Environmental Institute, there are about fifty-four of these groups in Brazil, but FUNAI has confirmed the existence of only twelve.

Intermittent contact: These are people who live in sparsely populated areas like the Amazon and the Center-West. Although they have been reached by the pioneering frontiers, they are mainly free from incursions because of government protection.

Permanent contact: These groups conserve certain elements of their ancestral tradition, such as language and culture. Yet they depend on a supply of goods from "civilization," which they have become used to and don't want to give up.

Integrated: These groups have lost their language and other racial characteristics but still maintain strong ties with and are loyal to their indigenous identity. They are economically dependent on the society in which they are stranded but struggle to preserve their land and their status as Indians.

Source: Povos renascidos—*Subsídios didáticos sobre a questão indígena*, serie B., vol. 1, Cimi-CNBB.

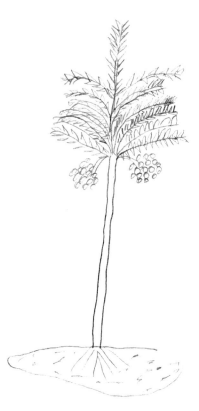

CLAUDINEIA AKAY

ILMA AKAI

Everyday Life
in the Village

[3]

Chronicles
and Testimonies

My Story

I, Daniel Monteiro Costa (Daniel Munduruku), was born in the city of Belém in the state of Pará in 1964. It was a time when people feared a military overthrow of the state—a very sad time in Brazil's history, when people were persecuted for having different ideas than the military. I was born Indian and grew up as an Indian, and I went to school in Belém.

When I was a small child, I often visited a village on the outskirts of the city. There I was lulled by the beautiful stories of my grandparents, aunts and uncles. Unfortunately, my parents, brothers and sisters and I can scarcely recall some of these stories. They have been lost in time, which is what happens to stories that are not told often enough.

From the age of seven to fifteen, I went to a Salesian School run by the Catholic Church, where I learned to love sports, especially soccer. I also developed a great love for children who were poor and marginalized, since my own family was very insecure economically. I also worked from an early age, selling candy, chips, shopping bags, ice cream and popsicles.

I was an Indian but I didn't like to be called one. I was ashamed, because people said that Indians were lazy and dirty.

I joined the Salesian Order wanting to become a priest. This experience took up six agreeable years of my life. I had time to rethink my personal goals, confront my indigenous identity and study philosophy. I had the chance to study in Manaus and work in Porto Velho, where I got to know people from other indigenous groups and became friends with people from different cultures. I got involved in projects helping street kids—projects that influenced my values and my personal choices.

In 1985 I left the Salesian Order because I realized that I needed to follow a path more related to my indigenous culture. In 1986 I settled in Manaus, a beautiful city on the banks of the Negro River, where I taught in a rural school set up especially for Indians.

In 1987, after finishing my B.A. in philosophy, I decided to move to the state of São Paulo to work and study. There I worked with homeless children, and for a short time I was a reporter and coordinator of an indigenous paper called *Guaypacare*.

At the end of 1989 I moved to the city of São Paulo, where I worked with street kids. By this time I had already met the person who would change my life—Tania Mara. Tania, who studied in the same faculty, always encouraged me to write and gave me lots of support. We were married in June 1990.

Since then I have continued to study, doing research on the Munduruku, my people, and to write. About what? Many things, but what I love most is to write the stories, the myths that indigenous people tell.

I dream about the end of racial, religious and political discrimination in Brazil. However, what I would like most is for there to be no more social discrimination. I don't want there to be so few rich people with tables overflowing with food and so many poor people who don't even have a table. If I had some magic power, my first act would be to change this situation. I would also give special attention to my Indian relatives, who have suffered greatly from other people's preconceptions and disrespect.

Childhood

When I was a five-year-old boy, my grandfather would sit me on his lap and tell me the stories of my people. I was dazzled by the intensity of his husky voice softened with time. With remarkable conviction he would tell the stories that explained the origins of our people and the vision of the universe.

I was always moved by the timelessness of the narrative. We would sit on the ground in front of the house and sometimes would only get up when the sun greeted us in the morning. How many times I wandered among the stars, lulled by the music in the tales of my old grandfather. How many times I was taken to the far-off limits of the universe to imagine myself as the hero of my people.

So many years later, toughened by my contact with other cultures, I still reflect about what I saw and lived through then. And I remember my grandfather's stories quietly and with great longing.

Today I can see that the stories that the old man told were his own dreams—dreams that perhaps said nothing about our external world but said a lot about the huge world that lies

deep inside us. I learned later that the stories weren't true. But I often came across people who cried because of them and, oddly, this crying made them true!

Now I know about science's frustrated attempts to map the cosmos and I realize that those ancient myths say what cannot be said. They are pure poetry, and through them I see how an identity can be created in the oral tradition.

If someone wants to understand my culture, they should read our stories, empathize with our heroes, experience our poetry!

What Do You Do With Mosquitoes?

When I was studying to be a teacher, I came in contact with people from very different backgrounds, who had very different views about indigenous people. Some said that the Indians were the true Brazilians and that the whites were guilty of barbarities against the indigenous groups who had disappeared. Others said they couldn't understand how Indians had remained so "backward," without education or technology. Still others took the middle ground, or had no opinion at all.

I remember sitting in the teachers' staff room with three other teachers, when suddenly they began talking about Indians.

"It must be really good being Indian," one teacher said. "But one thing puzzles me. What do Indians do with mosquitoes?"

"They smoke them," responded another.

"They're used to it," said a third teacher.

This made me angry, so I said, "No, in fact, we eat them."

Laughter echoed around the room. The subject died.

I hoped that they would ask me more about it, but I had no such luck. The teachers returned to their reading. I saw that I was not helping the indigenous cause by letting people believe that what I had said was true. In this case, I suppose I had the authority of the moment, and whatever I said would have been accepted. But I regretted it.

Education and Art

With my people I learned the real meaning of the word education. I would watch parents leading their children through the culture step by step. Fishing, hunting, making bows and arrows, cleaning fish, cooking, fetching water, felling trees. At night we would lie quietly and gaze up at the stars, trying to imagine the immense universe around us, the one that our pajés visited in their dreams.

I understood that educating someone meant teaching them how to dream. I learned to be Indian, then I learned to dream, or travel, to other realities. I passed

through them and learned from them. I learned to move from the inside out, to bring forth my dreams.

But I was disappointed to discover that in western society teachers did not usually guide children from the inside out. Instead, teachers brought the outside in, making children listen to heaps of unnecessary nonsense, while leaving their dreams stuck inside them. Children had no time to dream, and that is why they found school so boring.

I didn't choose to be Indian. That is a condition that was imposed on me by the divine mother who rules the universe. But I did choose to be a teacher. I want to tell my dreams so they can inspire other people to tell theirs...

Do Indians Eat People?

When I arrived in the state of São Paulo in 1987, I went to live in Lorena, a lovely town in the interior, in order to finish my course in philosophy at Salesiana College. At the beginning it was very difficult to find work.

Because I had experience working with young people, I got a job taking care of a group of children. It was satisfying. Children are very honest and don't hide their curiosity.

After introducing myself, I could see that they were full of amazement and curiosity. So I started to talk. And they asked questions.

"Hey, is it true that Indians only eat grass?" asked little Daniel.

"No, Daniel, it's not true. In fact, Indians don't like grass. They are more used to eating things like game, corn meal, cassava."

"But I'm not talking about grass," Daniel protested. "I'm talking about the bush itself."

"Do you think I have a face like a horse, Daniel?" I said in dismay. "You shouldn't believe everything you hear."

I convinced the boy. He eventually became my friend.

Then Diocleciano, Daniel's younger brother, asked, "Have you killed a lot of animals there in the bush?"

"Yes, I have," I said.

"Don't you know that it's bad to kill innocent animals?"

The question upset me. I tried to explain the different forms of survival and describe various ways of looking at hunting. I don't think Diocleciano heard anything I said, because since then he has never stopped telling me that it's bad to kill animals.

As I answered many more questions and promised to take the children to my village, I noticed a boy named André. He stood at the back of the room, very withdrawn. I went up to him, trying to get him to come closer, but he ran away from me.

The next day he returned with his mother. She told me that the boy had been deeply affected by my presence. He wanted to ask me a question, but he was afraid.

I tried to get him to ask me his question. After a little while, he beckoned me to lean over and asked, "Is it true that Indians eat people? What do they taste like? Did you kill the person first yourself? Was it a child or an adult? Did it taste like beef? Didn't it make you sick?"

André didn't want to hear my answer. He ran off, pointing his finger at me and repeating to his classmates, "Indians eat people. Indians eat people. Indians eat people."

Talking to Children

I am often invited to give speeches to children in schools in São Paulo, and it is always a learning experience for me.

Before one of these talks, a teacher came up and said that some of the children were frightened to learn that a "real" Indian was going to speak to them. When I went to the lecture hall, I could see that the children were nervous. Some were even hiding behind their teachers.

When they saw that I was dressed just like they were and that I didn't present any threat, a pupil came out from behind a teacher and said, "This is the one who's an Indian? Dressed like that? Oh, okay, I'm not afraid of him."

The audience burst out laughing. It was a perfect cue to begin my discussion with them.

THE CITY

When I first moved to the city, a number of really amazing encounters took place. I will present them to you as they happened. You can decide yourself what to think.

Are You Indian or Not?

When I first arrived in São Paulo, I enjoyed traveling by subway and bus. I especially liked to see the reactions of people when they saw me. I wanted them to know I was an Indian.

One day two women looked me up and

down when I entered the subway going to Place de Sé.

"Did you see that boy? He looks like an Indian," said one woman.

"He looks like it. But I'm not sure. He's wearing jeans. How can an Indian be wearing white clothing?"

"But did you see his hair? It's smooth, very smooth. Only Indians have hair like that. I think he is Indian."

"No, he isn't," the second woman protested. "Don't you see that he's wearing a watch? Indians tell time by looking at the sky. The watch of the Indian is the sun, the moon, the stars. He can't be an Indian."

"But he has squinty eyes," said the first woman.

"He's wearing shoes and a shirt."

"But his cheekbones are very prominent. Only Indians have cheekbones like that. No, he must be an Indian, and, it seems, a pure one."

"There are no more pure Indians," stated the second woman knowingly. "Anyway, how could an Indian be walking around the subway? Real Indians live in the forest, carry bows and arrows, hunt and fish and plant cassava."

"Did you see the necklace he's wearing? It looks like teeth. Could it be made of human teeth?"

"You're right, they are teeth! I've heard that there are still Indians who eat people."

"Didn't you say that you didn't think he was Indian? And now you're afraid he is one. Why don't we just ask him?"

"And if he doesn't like it?"

"Let's try. At least we would have better information, wouldn't we?"

"I'll ask."

I listened to this conversation between the two women and occasionally I laughed heartily. Suddenly I felt a light touch of fingers on my shoulder. I turned around. Unfortunately, they had waited too long to talk to me. Mine was the next stop.

I looked at them, smiled and said, "Yes!"

Japanese, Chilean or Indian?

Many people have a hard time starting a conversation with an Indian. This is what often happens when someone decides to talk to me on the street.

A person comes up to me and asks, "Are you Japanese?"

"No," I say.

"You look a lot like a Japanese friend of mine. In fact, he's Korean, but you look so much like him that I thought you were brothers. Are you sure that you don't know Mizaka?"

"No, I don't."

"If you're not Japanese, then you must be Chilean. Do you speak Spanish, man? I studied a little Spanish in school. Usted habla español?"

I say nothing. Finally my interrogator says to me, "If you're not Japanese or Chilean, then you must be Indian. You're Indian, aren't you?"

I nod. He starts talking again.

"I knew from the beginning, but I was embarrassed

to ask. Did you know that I'm also a descendant of Indians? My grandfather was pure Indian. He had a lasso. My mother says that my grandfather lived in the bush even. He was a real savage. It is you who are the real owners of Brazil. We are the invaders. I don't understand how people could want to get rid of the Indians. Do you live in the bush? Does that necklace have any meaning?"

After this avalanche of questions he patted me on the back, said goodbye and added that it was good to get to know me. But his ignorance continued just the same.

Whose God?

I often go to visit my Guarani relatives in a small village in Parelheiros, in São Paulo. I have enjoyed lots of parties and celebrations there. The Guarani people like sports and they are cheerful and happy, even though they live close together on only twenty-five acres of reserved land.

One January I attended a special Indian ceremony there. We spent a wonderful night dancing, singing, smoking and listening to the voices of the gods, who were speaking through the pajé. We talked about politics and the future of the indigenous people in the country. We talked right through until morning.

The next afternoon we heard that a Christian group had come to the village to pray. The village leader sent someone to ask them to leave, since there was no authorization for the group to enter the reserved area.

The messenger went to the group's pastor and told him the Guarani leader's decision.

The pastor came to try to convince us to let them stay. He began to talk to us, using Christian arguments, and it was hard to ignore what he was saying. One man began to defend Guarani culture. Some were threatening the pastor with bow and arrow.

Then Olívio, a Guarani who was taking philosophy at the University of São Paulo, began to argue with the pastor.

"You have no right to come here and pray in the name of a god who is already dead," Olívio said. "We follow a living god who offers us life."

"That's a lie," said the pastor. "You are ignorant. Our god is capable of giving salvation to yours. That is why we are here, to pray at the door that should be opened for salvation."

"Fortunately, we don't need to believe in this thing you call salvation," Olívio answered. "We can see that you don't understand anything about praying. You need to read more. Study philosophy. There are a great many white thinkers who disagree with you. Nietzsche said that this god that you pray to is dead, and it was you who killed him. Go away. It's the best thing you can do."

I think Olívio won the debate more with his angry defense of Guarani culture than with Nietzsche's ideas. In any case, the pastor never returned to the village— thanks, perhaps, to the slender Guarani named Olívio.

My Hope

At the end of this book I would like to make a plea—to put the rights of the child into practice. If you don't know what these are, go to the nearest library and find out and then teach them to your brothers and sisters. Then bring together your friends and your friends' friends and tell them about children's rights. Then bring together all adults who love children and together shout very loudly, "I have the right to be a child!"

Glossary

aguti - A rodent related to the guinea pig, but with longer legs.

cassava - A tropical plant with starchy, nutritious roots that is a staple of the indigenous people in Brazil.

cauxi - The Munduruku word for bad spirits that inhabit sick people's bodies.

embira - Hemp-like fibers used for making nets and ropes.

exogamous - Marriage outside a specific tribe or social unit.

FUNAI - The Brazilian Federal Agency for Indian Affairs.

indigenous - Originating in and characterizing a particular country or region; native.

Mário Juruna - The first Indian to be elected to the federal parliament in Brazil. Mr. Juruna became well known after he tape-recorded promises government officials made to his people and was able to prove that they were being lied to.

ku - The Munduruku word for the traditional small parcel of land used to cultivate food.

pajé - The Portuguese word for traditional healer, shaman, medicine man.

pariwat - The Munduruku word for white people.

shaman - A traditional medicine man or, often, both a traditional healer and a religious leader, as Karu Bempô and Kaxi are.

tapir - A pig-like animal, related to the rhinoceros, that has a long flexible snout.

Suggestions for Further Reading

Books marked with an asterisk (*) are of particular interest to young readers.

*Bender, Evelyn. *Brazil.* Philadelphia, PA: Chelsea House, 1999. An overview of Brazil's history, culture and politics.

Descola, Philippe. *The Spears of Twilight: Life and Death in the Amazon Jungle.* New York: New Press, 1993. The author spent three years among the Javaro Indians of the Upper Amazon. He presents their daily life, their joys and sorrows, their songs, their magical encounters with the spirits of their ancestors.

*Gheerbrant, Alain. *The Amazon: Past, Present and Future.* Translated from French by I. Mark Paris. New York: Harry Abrams, 1992. A fascinating book full of archival documents, drawings and photos that trace the history of the Amazon since 1542, when two Spanish conquistadors "discovered" the mystical world of the Amazon and its inhabitants.

*Heinrichs, Ann. *Brazil: Enchantment of the World,* Second Series. New York: Children's Press, 1993. Describes the geography, plants, animals, history, economy, culture and people of Brazil.

Hemming, John. *Red Gold: The Conquest of the Brazilian Indians, 1500-1760.* Cambridge: Harvard University Press, 1978. A history of the colonial conquest of the Native peoples of Brazil.

*Lewington, Anna. *Rain Forest Amerindians.* Austin: Raintree Steck-Vaughn Publishers, 1993. Outlines the problems of Amazon's indigenous people and their struggles to protect their land, maintain their culture and improve their economic status.

Meggers, Betty J. *Amazonia. Man and Culture in a Counterfeit Paradise.* rev. ed. Washington and London: Smithsonian Institute, 1996. A revised edition of one of the first comprehensive books on the Amazon and its people.

* Plotkin, Mark J. *Tales of a Shaman's Apprentice.* New York: Viking Penguin, 1993. Describes scientist Mark Plotkin's ten years living with indigenous people in the Amazon to learn about native plants and their use as medicines.

*Reynolds, Jan. *Amazon Basin. Vanishing Cultures*. New York: Harcourt Brace, 1993. A photo-essay showing a day in the village life of Yanomana Indians in the Amazon rain forest.

Roosevelt, Anna, ed. *Amazonian Indians from Prehistory to the Present: Anthropological Perspectives*. Tucson: University of Arizona Press, 1994. An anthology of articles about the Amazon Indians, including social life and customs, history and economy, with a bibliography and index.

Index